Thirst

THIRST

A Story of a German ISIS Member & Her Yazidi Victim

A novel based on true events

SUZAN KHAIRI

Westphalia Press
An Imprint of the Policy Studies Organization
Washington, DC
2024

Thirst: A Story of a German
ISIS Member & Her Yazidi Victim

All Rights Reserved © 2024 by Policy Studies Organization

Westphalia Press
An imprint of Policy Studies Organization
1367 Connecticut Avenue NW
Washington, D.C. 20036
info@ipsonet.org

ISBN: 978-1-63723-848-6

Daniel Gutierrez-Sandoval, Executive Director
PSO and Westphalia Press

Updated material and comments on this edition
can be found at the Westphalia Press website:
www.westphaliapress.org

To Rania, whose memory lives on in these pages.

"This world is a colourful place, full of many people, religions and forces, but each of them worships God in their own way, and each of them sees God with their own eyes."

~ Proverb about peace and coexistence
in the Yazidi religion

FOREWORD

This novel, written by Suzan Khairi, which is based on true events about the plight of the minority Yazidi community in Iraq, is heart wrenching. It is a story about how ISIS snatched away in a swift moment a centuries-old community's unique, beautiful, serene, and peaceful way of life—a community without rancor or malice in its heart, a community that embraced nature and found all the comfort and solace that only the virtuous and benevolent are blessed to enjoy and relish. Suzan's story crystallizes the horror that has been inflicted by ISIS on these most peaceful and beautiful humans being that have lived on the same land for centuries. They have contributed silently and in an unassuming way to the beauty of the human spirit and its revelation when left to roam free and sway like a flower in the gentle breeze.

The Yazidis, an ethnic and religious minority in Iraq, have tragically faced severe persecution during the war against ISIS, which began around 2014. ISIS targeted them specifically because of their religious beliefs, leading to mass killings, kidnappings, enslavement, and other atrocities. Many Yazidis were forced to flee their homes, particularly from the Sinjar region.

Currently the situation for Yazidis is still challenging. While ISIS no longer holds significant territory in Iraq, the aftermath of their persecution has left deep scars. Thousands of Yazidi women and girls remain missing, and while the process of finding them and reuniting them with their families continues, it is at a glacial pace. Many Yazidis remain displaced, living in camps with limited access to basic services. Others live precariously in Europe, with those whose asylum claims have been rejected facing deportation back to Iraq, which is still unsafe for them. Rebuilding their communities and returning to their home is a slow process, hindered by security concerns and a lack of resources.

The international community can and indeed must do all it can to help alleviate the Yazidis' suffering and bring the perpetrators of genocide to justice. It is critical to provide humanitarian aid, including basic necessities like food, shelter, and medical care, especially for those living in displaced persons camps. In addition, the Yazidis need psychological support to help cope with the extreme trauma they have endured. Adding to that, it is necessary to invest in infrastructure and rebuild homes, schools, and other essential structures, as to enable them to return and rebuild their lives.

Of great importance is to protect them from further attacks, and resolving local conflicts is necessary for a safe return to their homeland. And yes, it will be necessary to hold ISIS accountable for their crimes against the Yazidis, including international legal proceedings, which are important for justice and closure. Some of these measures are indeed taking place, but the process has been needlessly slow and only prolongs the Yazidis' suffering.

It is sadder than sad that only human beings are capable of committing atrocities that even the most vicious of all beasts would not crave. Suzan's story is a reminder to all people of conscience to never rest until we arrest the vicious cycle of egregious human rights violations wherever they may occur. Moral virtues are human; if we don't rise to protect them, we lose our humanity.

~ Alon Ben-Meir

October 25, 2021
Munich

A woman dressed in black entered the Munich court, bending as if the guilt of the whole world was on her shoulders, covering her face with a file of papers, trying to cover up from the camera lenses to hide her features from people's eyes while she is in front of five judges with sharp features and firm words to determine her fate. This atmosphere took a woman away from the crowd; she had a pale face with prominent lines that made her look decades older than her age. The sadness appeared on her, and her heart was squeezed with pain. She closed her big eyes, remembering the festival day eight years ago, August the 2nd, as if the past had risen before her eyes in a little village named Kocho, located in Iraq, as a small family whose father and mother are orphans, gathered for a meal, eating breakfast consisting of well-fermented black tea, goat's milk, and hot bread, or what they call *Naan*, in the kitchen of their tiny house. They were sitting on a piece of cloth on the ground while enjoying the air of the electric fan on that hot morning. The little girl got very excited as she ate the milk, and happiness overwhelmed her. Her little brother almost burst out laughing, so his parents laughed with him as they looked at her eating greedily as if it was her last meal.

Her father said, laughing while wiping her mouth with a handkerchief:

"My spoiled little girl, be patient, and don't eat so quickly, you will get sick, and your father will not bear to see you in pain."

And laughter echoed in their small house, filled with the spirit of festival, happiness, roses, and sweet smells. They are dressed in festival clothes to roam the village among relatives and friends despite their fear and concern about the control of a terrorist organization called ISIS over most of the neighboring areas of the village. But this bitter reality did not stop them from enjoying this holiday, and they wandered around the village while laughter and the sound of music rose in the sky, and the children were happy with what they had collected of sweets and money. Until it got dark, and the moon rose from behind the horizon, they returned to their house and got ready for bed. But after their mother slept, the two children had another opinion because they did not want to sleep, and they embraced their father while looking at his calm face, begging him to play with them, but he was too tired to play, as he is a man approaching his forties, but he did not want the sorrows of his children, so he got up from his bed with enthusiasm and carried them while tickling them, and he said in a low register, like the voice of a cartoon reader, as he took them to their bed:

"If you want to watch a shadow play, raise your hand!"

They laughed and raised their hands, repeating: "We do...," but the father acted as if he did not hear a thing and said: "I cannot hear anyone! I thought there were children who wanted to! I will go to sleep then." The kids shouted "We are here, and we want to. Can't you see us?"

Their father laughed and said, "It's as if I'm hearing the voice of two children who want to do it, and they are my spoiled children. Get ready, folks, the best play ever is going to begin."

The two children sat quietly on their beds, and their father started the shadow play and said:

"Once upon a time, there was a large ewe who lived in a mud hut with seven young sheep," as he formed shapes with his hands indicating sheep, "they pushed one another to get milk from their mother."

Dalal asked her father in astonishment, "But why don't they ask someone else for milk?!"

Her father replied, "Be patient a little. You will know that at the end of the story." And he continued the story, saying, "This beautiful ewe was taking care of them and preparing food for them every day. One day, she went to the forest to bring food for them, but she was afraid the wolf would come to eat them while she was gone, so she warned them: "I am going to the forest to bring you food, my little ones, but beware of the wolf as he may come while I am gone and ask you to open the door, so do not listen to what he says, the wolf has an ugly, scary, and hoarse voice, and he has two black legs with thick hair. If he comes to you, recognize him from these features." The children answered her: "We will take care of the evil wolf, mother, and we will not allow him to deceive us and eat us. You can go to the forest safely." The mother agreed and left for the forest while her children stayed back home alone. Suddenly, they heard someone knocking on their door and saying: "Open the door for me, my children, I returned from the forest and brought you delicious food. Come one, open up." The little sheep stood behind the door listening carefully to the voice, and said: "Go away, you have a hoarse voice; you are the evil wolf and not our mother. Our mother has a soft and beautiful voice." The wolf went to a nearby shop and brought some honey, and ate it, thinking that it would change his hoarse voice. He went back to the sheep again, asking them: "Open the door, my little ones, I am your mother," but the smart sheep looked from under the door and found two scary legs covered with black hair, so they said: "Go away, you evil one, you are not our mother. Our mother has two white legs, not like yours." The wolf went to the bakery and covered his body with flour, and returned to the sheep's house, saying: "Open the door, my beloved ones, I am your mother. I brought you the most delicious food." The sheep looked from under the door, saw the whiteness of the wolf's legs, and thought he was their mother, so they opened the door, and behold, there was a wolf in front of them."

The two kids got scared when they heard the story, and they screamed as if the wolf had entered their own house, so the father laughed and said, "Should I finish the story or not?"

They fearful responded, "Yeah, we're enjoying the story."

He continued: "The sheep got scared a lot and ran all over the house to hide from the evil wolf. Some hid behind the door, some hurried to the wardrobe, and another under the bed, but the wolf found them all and ate them, except for a little sheep hiding in a clock hanging on the wall. After that, the wolf came out of the house tired, sat under a tree, and fell into a deep sleep. The poor mother ewe returned to see the door of the house open. She looked for her children, but she did not find any of them, so she began crying for them with a burning heart. The little sheep came out of the clock when he heard his mother's voice. And he told her everything that happened. The mother went to look for the wolf and found him sleeping under the tree with his stomach moving. She realized that her children were alive in the stomach of the evil wolf. So she brought a scissors, cut his belly, and took her children out of it. Then, she replaced them with stones and sewed the wolf's belly. The next day, the wolf woke up thirsty and went to the river to drink, but he fell into it from the weight of the stones in his stomach, and the evil wolf died, and the seven sheep lived with their mother safely."

The girl said happily, "I love the mother ewe very much, she is very brave."

Her father responded while looking at her angelic face: "I will protect you and your brother like this sheep, but now you must sleep. It is already ten o'clock in the evening!"

So the two children got ready for sleep, and their father went to his small room next to his wife and hugged her while she was asleep. She woke up from her deep sleep, almost unable to open her eyes, and asked him: "Did the children sleep, Shivan?"

He replied with features dominated by expressions of concern, "My love, don't worry, they are asleep and safe." He was worried about his family due to what had happened in the places surrounding their village, and he thought about what might happen to them until he fell into a deep sleep.

PART I
MURDER

August 3, 2014
3:00 AM, Kocho

Amidst the panic and screams of the villagers, Shivan woke up and quickly went to his children's room to check on them after he checked on his wife. He looked at his children: Dalal, five years old, with an angelic face and silky black hair like her mother's, and Meer, nine years old, with a calm face and soft features, and he said to himself, "I have experienced the summer and winter of life, and I have stood before many storms, this is one of them, and I will come out of it peacefully."

As for Noor, she was silent, looking at Shivan one time and at her two children another, as if she was seeing the beginning of a chapter in their lives and the end of another chapter. She tiptoed quietly to her husband with a fearful but clear face and whispered in his ear: "What's going on in the village?! Are we safe here?"

Shivan replied, "My love, I don't know, but I will protect you no matter what it costs me, and I will not abandon you." He asked her to stay with the children so that he could see what was happening in the village, but he was not sure of his ability to protect his family, as he was a poor man with no authority and did not embrace a vital religion in the region. Rather, ISIS sees him as an atheist (kafir) who deserves death. He imagined many different scenarios, like a fantasy before his eyes, until he reached the house door. He saw many men, some shivering from the fear, and some seemed careless about the imminent danger that might befall them all. Shivan asked them worriedly, "What is going on here?"

One of them answered him: "ISIS!" and stopped so that another one said: "They say that ISIS entered the city and people from all villages are fleeing for their lives, but I do not know what is happening here. No one is moving from their place! They say that ISIS will not do anything to us."

Shivan replied while moving from one place to another: "Are you all crazy? It is a terrorist organization! How can you believe these lies!? Do you know what a terrorist organization means?! In the end, you are followers of the Yazidi religion!" pointing his finger at each person. He stood there and said: "You are all infidels and atheists in their eyes, and killing you is lawful! How do you believe this nonsense?!"

One of the men replied to him, saying, "Believe me, there is no danger to our village. This is what all the Arab clan heads in our neighboring villages said. They only took control of the ruling system in the region, and nothing will happen to us. Whoever left the village with the intention of fleeing will regret that; the danger to them is greater, so let us all stay in the village. We either die together or live together."

Shivan asked him about the number of people who left the village, and he replied, "About five hundred and forty people, including children and women, out of one thousand seven hundred and forty people, the population of the village."

Shivan remained silent, closed his eyes, and said to himself: "This is a war between religions, and we are the ones who will lose in it."

Shivan returned to his house, and he did not know what decision he should take to save his family. The more he thought, the faster he walked, and the more his anxiety grew. He was in a frightening conflict between his mind and his heart. He arrived at the door of his house, and he had decided to take his family and get out of the village, but he did not find them in the house, and there was news that ISIS had already entered the village, so he started screaming with all his might while calling for his wife, but in vain, so he rushed out of the house to the street, lost and not knowing where he to go, as if he was not in his village that he had always lived in and loved. It suddenly turned from a warm place with a bright sun full of roses' scent into a cold place dominated by darkness with a stinky smell, and life stopped in it until he saw a woman holding the hand of two children heading towards him, but he could not recognise her from a distance, because the atmosphere was dusty, and he was distracted and didn't see clearly until she approached him and said in her heavy voice, "My love, what happened to you? Are you okay?"

He embraced her, shocked, without saying a word, as he had thought that he had lost them forever.

10:00 AM

People felt the end is approaching, and fear has taken over the village. The forces of darkness and evil have headed towards the house of the village chief, carrying weapons, flames of revenge and killing in their eyes, and the smell of death emanating from them, dressed in black and almost unrecognizable due to their beards and long hair, in cars covered in dust and mud. After their groups seized control of all the other villages in the city and committed massacres against innocent people, they stood in front of his house door and sat silently in his hall, without any coffee offered or laughter heard.

The village chief struck the table in front of him with his hand, looking at their gloomy faces, and said loudly: "We have nothing to offer you in this village, so please return to where you came from." With a quick glance, the ISIS member looked at him, hatred in his eyes, and slowly said: "We did not come to harm you, but to liberate your village, like the other villages, from the oppression you were subjected to, and let it be known that all the other villages are now out of the hands of the infidels and under our control." Another member said, "We also entered another village today, and all the people of the village are there, which is adjacent to yours." The chief asked, "What was its name?" A third member said: "Al-Hatemiyah."

A sound came from behind the door, and everyone turned to see another ISIS member with a wicked appearance, dark circles around his eyes, a long beard, and a trimmed moustache. He said loudly with intense hatred, "Enough of this nonsense! Ask everyone in your village to surrender their weapons, or else death will be your fate. We have warned you, but those who disobey our orders will face death, and those who comply with us are safe, except for police and military personnel whose fate is already sealed. Inform everyone in the village to stay in their homes and not to move from their places."

The fear overtook the village chief, not for himself or his family, but for the villagers. How could he deliver such a message knowing that these people were nothing but evil? However, he summoned his courage and replied, "Your message will reach the people, and no one will disobey your orders."

The ISIS member replied, "We will see if the Yazidi is a man of his word or not." He paused for a moment before turning to his group and said, "We have said everything we have to say. Let's go now, and we will be back soon."

The village chief looked at the clock, realizing that time was passing without any message reaching the villagers. He did not know what to do to save them. Escape would lead to inevitable death while staying meant an unknown fate. After consulting with those around him, he decided to deliver the message to everyone in the village, as they had the right to know what was happening.

After everyone in the village, including Shivan and his family, received the ISIS message, they had to take a difficult decision. However, they thought that staying was the best solution, as the ISIS member had stated that those who complied with their orders would not be harmed.

The people, and even the animals and birds, hid in their homes as silence and darkness descended upon the village.

Morning turned into night in their eyes, and they could think of nothing but a terrifying fate and impending death.

At that moment, a strong wind swept through the village, bringing a thick cloud of dust that made the village even darker in the morning. The voice of evil Caliphate and leader of ISIS, Abu Bakr al-Baghdadi, echoed in every house of the village as he delivered his sermon; they were listening to the man who was going to decide their fate reciting his speech "Friday Sermon and Prayer in the Great Mosque of Mosul for our Leader and Commander, May God Preserve Him." This sermon was released as an audio recording after the capture of Mosul by ISIS on June 10, 2014, in which he declared himself as Caliphate of the Muslims and ascended the pulpit of the historic al-Nuri Mosque.

In the sermon, a man dressed in a black robe and turban appeared on the pulpit, seeming to suffer from a leg injury and placing his left hand under his robe. He raised a black flag with a white circle inside it, on which it was written in black: "Allah, the Messenger, Muhammad." Above the circle, it was written in white: "There is no god but Allah." He called on his followers to obey him and to pledge allegiance to him, describing his leadership as a great responsibility and a heavy trust. He called on all Muslims around the world to take up arms and gather in the Islamic State in Iraq and Syria and to continue their jihad to establish Islam.

He cited Quranic verses and praised the virtues of jihad, emphasizing the necessity of fighting the atheists and establishing Sharia law and its punishments. In his opinion, these goals can only be achieved through force and authority, and the backbone of religion is a book that guides and a sword that conquers. He promised his followers that if they spread the religion of Islam on earth and fought for its cause, they would be rewarded with many good deeds that would enter them into paradise, for Allah is with them and will give them victory.

3:00 PM

Shivan heard a strong movement outside, so he listened fearfully as the sound of cars on the street approached his house and parked. He held his breath and waited behind the door, his heart trembling and his emotions disturbed, as he heard the car doors open and closed, followed by footsteps approaching his house bit by bit. Then, suddenly, one of them knocked on the door with great force, causing him to step back, shivering.

A loud knocking on the door was heard by Noor, so she guessed what was happening. She got up from her place while holding her children and took them to hide in the old wardrobe that was in her room, hoping that they would be safe from any harm that might happen to them.

Surrendering himself to God, Shivan opened the door, and when he did, he saw three people, and he recognized their appearance as belonging to the terrorist organization of ISIS. Their leader approached him and asked him to surrender any weapons in the house, threatening him with death if he didn't comply.

He replied, trembling, "I am a poor man and do not have any weapons."

But the leader did not believe him and ordered his men to search his house thoroughly while he pleaded with them not to harm his children and wife. But they threw him on the ground and entered the house, searching room after room.

One of them stared at the wardrobe and said loudly, while laughing, "The big surprise is in this wardrobe!"

Noor panicked and silently prayed to God to keep her and her family safe from them! It wasn't long until the ISIS member opened the wardrobe, grabbed her and her children by force, and asked them to stand and face the wall with her husband. If they didn't obey their orders, they would face the consequences. They whipped their backs with a lash in front of the children, repeating, "You infidels, you cowards."

Their leader turned to them and ordered them to stop what they were doing and leave the house to complete their mission.

After they left the house, the two children began to cry, having endured the silence under intense fear and sadness. The mother ran to hug them while the father fell to his knees, a desperate man feeling a fire burning in his back from the severe beating.

Shivan looked at his wife and children in that state, remembering everything that was happening in the village and their inability to leave it. He felt as if all the doors were closed in front of him, so his chest tightened, and he rose silently and went to the bathroom. He turned on the water, put his hand over his mouth, and cried loudly as if he were in a large, lifeless cemetery with no life.

Days passed, and the commotion of ISIS calmed down in the village, and the residents breathed a sigh of relief. They began to talk among themselves that ISIS would not cause any harm to civilians, and it had been a long time since they had come to the village. But soon, tension returned to them after the news spread in the village of the new request from ISIS to the residents of the two villages, Kocho and

Al-Hatimiyah, to declare their conversion to Islam. They said that they would treat them like other Muslims under their law, or else their fate would be death. However, they asked ISIS for a period of five days, thinking that someone would save them. The world as a whole would not stand idly by and just watch. After numerous consultations, ISIS gave them a period of five days to convince the residents of the two villages and placed them under strict guard to prevent them from escaping.

There was a conversation between the chiefs of the two villages over the phone, where the chief of Al-Hatimiyah asked the other to put a plan in place to escape, saying in a low and tense voice, "They asked us to convert to Islam! This is an impossible demand! No one in the village will agree to it, and I will not allow anyone in my village to be killed!"

The other replied, "But it's not that easy! How can we get all the people out of the village while it's under constant surveillance?"

The chief of Al-Hatimiyah replied, "We will find a solution! To die trying is better than dying while standing helpless!"

The chief of Kocho replied, "What about the children and women? Our village is under tight guard! They are more focused on us than you and don't forget that you are closer to the mountain than we are. We cannot escape as we are very far away."

The other chief responded, "I don't know what to say to you! But I won't just stand here facing an unknown fate. Finally, I ask God to be with you."

The chief of KhoCho said with great sadness, "May God be with us all in any decision we make." And the call ended.

On the night of the fourth day of the deadline, all the residents of Al-Hatimiyah village woke up as if they were heading to their graves on that dark night. At the chief's request, they prepared to leave in silence and head towards the mountain in Shingal (Sinjar), where many Yazidis from all other villages took refuge to escape from ISIS, as it was the only place that ISIS could not enter in the entire city. They left all the lights, generators, and other electrical devices on to avoid suspicion of their absence from their homes.

The escape of the village residents was not noticed until morning came. After they discovered what had happened, dozens of cars filled with ISIS militants roamed the village of Kocho. They had gone crazy, as a part of their prey had escaped from their hands, and they started firing into the air, speaking in a more violent tone than before, and making death threats. People stayed silent behind the doors of their homes, waiting with great fear for what was to come.

Under strict guard, a long night passed over the village like an endless nightmare. In every home, a mother comforted her children by saying that tomorrow would be better, the sun would rise again, and sweet and beautiful dreams would come to them, unafraid of the darkness of the night. And a desperate father looking at his family, who are in grave danger, without being able to help them. And an old woman afraid for her religion and beliefs that she had always believed in and wished to die with. And a child confused, unable to read the faces of the adults and understand what was happening between them.

August 15, 2014
11:00 AM, Kocho

Someone knocked lightly on Shivan's door so as not to make any noise. Shivan stood up trembling and asked his wife not to follow him. It was his neighbour who lived nearby. He was surprised and looked at him carefully. He saw a person who was smiling and happy in those days when no one knew the meaning of happiness. The man said excitedly, "We have been saved, my neighbour! Everyone in the village is getting ready to go to the mountain. ISIS has granted us amnesty and said they would treat us like Christians. We just have to pay the Jizya tax."

Shivan was even more surprised and asked, "Who said that? Are you sure of this news?" The man replied, "Yes, they asked all the villagers to go to the village school, it's big enough for us to gather, and then they will take us all to the mountain." Shivan said, "I'll tell my wife and kids, and we'll join you."

He went into the house, still unsure of what to do. But he wanted to believe what was happening at that moment, so he went to his wife and hugged her tightly, saying, "I will hug you and my children in a way that I will never forget, even after a hundred years." He sat down next to them and stared at their faces carefully while they looked at him in amazement.

His wife asked nervously, "What's happening here? Why are you hugging us as if you'll never see us again?" Shivan smiled, tears in his eyes, and said, "No, it's joy, not sadness! Everyone in the village has been granted amnesty, and they will take us to the mountain to join the others. But now we must prepare to go to the village school, where everyone is gathering."

His little daughter jumped for joy from her mother's lap and held her father's hand, saying with an angelic smile and innocent eyes, "Let's go to the mountain, Daddy! Do you know that it's my life's dream to see the mountain? I've only seen it on TV." Her father replied with a heart full of doubt, "I'll take my only daughter to the mountain, and we'll have a barbecue party there." She said excitedly, "And the little animals and birds will join our party too, won't they?"

Smiling, her father replied, "Yes, the small animals will also take part in it."

"And the birds?!" the girl responded sadly.

"And the birds too! How can I forget them? Now, get ready to go to school," her father answered.

After a few minutes, he went out with his family and headed towards the village school. Everyone was walking in that direction, and the village was full of cars carrying armed members of ISIS, holding the flag of the caliphate.

He trembled as he walked among them and heard the whispers of the militants, all of whom expressed admiration for the beauty of the village's women. His imaginary fear turned into real fear at that moment. However, he continued walking and whispered in his wife's ear, "Don't leave our children no matter what happens! They are your responsibility from this moment on."

Noor was also disturbed and asked fearfully, "Why would you say such a thing? Is there something you're hiding from me?!"

He didn't answer her, saying to himself, "Is this the beginning of our end? I hope I have the opportunity to fulfil my daughter's dream."

Shivan was avoiding the streets he once loved in the village, so he could remember them as they were before. He wasn't thinking of anything else, waiting to reach that school so they could go to the mountain after it.

At that terrible hour, Shivan arrived at the school gate, guarded by many militants in their strange attire. They asked them to enter quietly.

He entered and found a large hall on the ground floor with a staircase leading to the other floor, with an armed man on each step and a man with a camera next to them recording what was happening there. All the villagers were there under strict guard, and silence dominated the situation.

He had goosebumps and shivered as he had never felt terror and fear like this in his entire life, to the point where he felt his knees were incapable of holding him up. He closed his eyes, wondering about the dark fate that destiny had brought him to.

Five people came to that hall, and one of them, with a thick beard and an ugly face, introduced himself to the audience as Abu Hamza Al-Khatooni, an ISIS prince (Amir) with the order of the governor (Wali) of Mosul. With incomprehensible looks to everyone, he asked the other four to put down the black bags they were carrying on the ground and open them. He then asked everyone to put their gold, money, and phones in the bags as a ransom for their lives.

Shavan remained calm and did not allow himself to panic. He stared at his wedding ring and thought to himself, "Unbelievable things are happening in this world! Who would have thought that my wedding ring would one day save my life!" He asked his wife to give him everything she had, as he did not want her to get close to them, having heard that they take beautiful women for themselves.

His wife spoke softly, without raising her head, "What about Dalaal's earrings? She's very sad and does't want to give them up."

Shivan sat in front of his daughter, opened his hand in front of her, and smiled. Dalaal understood and placed her earrings in his hand, her face showing both anger and sadness. She said, "But you'll buy me better ones, right?"

"Of course, I will," her father replied.

They filled the bags with all their valuable belongings and carried them to the cars. They asked the women and children to go to another floor and wait there while the older women gathered in another large hall to the left of the main hall. The ISIS leader shouted, "The time has come. We will take the men to the mountain first, in groups, and each will wait his turn."

Shivan looked at his wife and children, his eyes filled with tears as they moved away from him. He felt sad and depressing emotions running through his body. He quickly left with others towards the trucks that were designated for their transportation, they drove east, passing by his house on the way. In that brief moment, he remembered everything he had experienced in that village, from the day he joined the school to the day he carried his children in his arms. He trembled a little, like a person who has seen death and does not know how long he will remain in that state. All he knew was that it was the unknown.

One man grabbed him forcefully by his shoulder while he was distracted and asked him to get off the truck. He hurried to get out and tremblingly said, "But we are still close to the village, and we haven't reached the mountain yet!"

The ISIS member laughed and replied, "We know that! We have decided to prepare a feast for you first, as we heard that you haven't eaten yet."

More than fifty armed, masked men dressed in black stood in a single line and made every young person raise their arms to check if they were mature (from the hair of their armpits). Those who did not have hair under their armpits were sent back to the trucks, while the others were ordered to lie down on the ground in batches. Some raised the black flag, and others took pictures with their cameras.

At that moment, everyone knew their fate was death. One of them tried to escape at that moment, hoping to save his life, but his chances of survival were as slim as a sheep trying to escape from fifty wolves. He ran towards the village at full speed without intending to stop, and as soon as he entered the village, he heard the shouts of "Allahu Akbar" echoing. He fell to the ground, was shot by more than ten bullets, and was killed.

The ISIS member shouted, "And so his miserable end came."

Shivan lay on the ground with the first batch, placing his

hands on his head, and said to himself, "So this is my story! I reached its end without having an end to it." That's how he thought, or rather, that's how he struggled to endure his fate, tears streaming from his eyes and a wild storm raging inside him. He remembered the past and compared it to the present until despair overtook him, and he cried uncontrollably, repeating his children's names over and over again.

Suddenly, voices emanated from the darkness, shouting, "Allahu Akbar ... Allahu Akbar." He felt two bullets penetrate his back and settle in his bowels, so he vomited blood. Another bullet pierced his skull, and everything around him turned into pitch darkness. He looked to his left and saw his children playing and running with their mother, their laughter ringing out, filled with happiness. However, every time he tried to approach them, they moved further and further away until he finally slept forever next to his fellow villagers, from whom only a few survived under the dead bodies.

PART II
SOUQ AL-SABAYA

3:11 PM, Kocho school

The sound of gunfire filled the village for almost an hour after the men were taken from the school. Noor's eyes widened in shock as the first shot was fired, and she whispered her husband's name in despair, saying, "Shivan! No, what I'm thinking can't be true."

The school became full of children crying out of fear and women's screams of grief, some shouting, "My children!" and others, "My husband! My brother!"

The gunmen cursed them and ordered them to be silent, or they would kill them all. Noor tightly covered her mouth with her hand to stifle her scream out of fear for her children. An ISIS member sneaked up behind her like a ghost, but she quickly felt his presence and turned around, clutching her children tightly with her hands. He grabbed her slender neck with his large hands, stared into her stunned and angry features, and scoffed, "Who comes after Allah?"

She bravely replied, "Tawus Malak, the Angel King."

He tightened his grip around her neck and raised the index finger of his other hand, saying, "The Prophet Mohammed is the one who comes after Allah."

"Kocho has always been an Yazidi village and will remain so forever," Noor replied.

The ISIS member screamed at her, calling her a cursed whore, and pushed her forcefully against the nearby wall, causing her to fall to the ground. She pressed her head against her children's out of fear. Another ISIS member then entered the room, walking confidently with a black gun raised high in his right hand. He looked to his left, where a slender man stood near the entrance, the village's chief. He approached him and stared at him for a moment before scratching his head with the gun's nozzle and raising his thick eyebrows, saying, "What are you doing here? Have you decided to abandon Satan's worship and worship the one, Allah?"

The chief shook his head with an expression of astonishment and said, "We already worship the one, God! And Tawus Malak is the angel whom God honored and made the head of the seven angels after he refused to prostrate to Adam, whom God created and asked the angels to prostrate to. Tawus said that prostration is for God alone and cannot be for anyone else. This was a test for the angels, and he was the only one to pass it. Therefore, we pray for his devotion to God and his eternal worship, and our story has nothing to do with what you say and believe in, and this is our belief. He paused briefly and continued, "We believe that good and evil come from within the human being, and everyone chooses their own path. Peace and humanity are our way, and that will never change."

The militant pointed the gun at the chief and ordered him to walk out before him, so he took him with the help of others to the vicinity of the school and ordered him to get on his knees and put his hands on his head so he surrendered to his inevitable fate and looked for the last time with a look of pity and sadness at his village that he spent his entire life serving. He closed his eyes forever, wishing that one day it would return to the way it was in the past. His body and head were filled with random bullets that were fired from the weapons.

The trucks came back to the school door, and one ISIS member yelled, "Start crying for yourselves, you whores!"

The place began to be filled with chaos, and the militants pushed the women into groups, and screams and insults erupted from both sides, and the school was filled with the smell of sweat mixed with fear and tears on that hot summer day.

They pushed them into the open trucks from the back, each truck carrying more than eighteen girls and children. Noor was in the second truck with her children. She sat in the back, clinging to her children in a narrow place, her shoulders touching the shoulders of the others, and the truck started moving quickly on the bumpy dirt road leading to the outside of the village. At first, she did not know where they were going. The last time she left the village was four months ago when she visited the Sinjar city center to shop for the Yazidi New Year's Day. There is everything a person needs in terms of clothes, food, various sweets, and colors for coloring eggs.

After half an hour, the truck entered a place crowded with people, and life was normal in it. As Noor raised her head to see the place from the truck's hatch, she remembered that place well, they were in Sinjar, so she asked herself about the reason for normal life in it as if nothing had happened! She began to comprehend while looking at the veiled women that they were the Muslims who remained in the city.

The truck moved away from Sinjar, heading east, and the truck hit a cement bump in the street hard, Dalal's head hit the edge of the truck, so she looked at her mother, placing her hand on the place where her head hit the truck with tears in her eyes as she bit her lower lip as if asking her permission to cry. Noor hugged her and told her nothing had happened to your head, the truck was the one that got hurt. This is a phrase used by Yazidi mothers to comfort their children so the little girl calm down.

The city began to disappear on the horizon. Before sunset, the truck stopped in front of a large dark building located in a strange place. Noor got out, holding her children's hands and joined the others in the courtyard in front of the building. She saw girls and children who had already disembarked before them, so she asked one of them, "Where are we?"

"We are in Soulagh, and this building is the Soulagh Institute," the girl replied.

Soulagh is a beautiful place, famous for its greenery and fresh water. Noor had heard a lot about it from her deceased father, who used to work in the nearby cement factory. But she couldn't believe what she saw; the place was dark and nothing like what everyone had said about it.

After all the trucks arrived, a member of ISIS came and forcefully opened the door of the institute, ordering everyone to enter it, but not before removing their scarves. All the women took off their scarves and threw them on the ground, feeling great pain in their hearts, while the children looked in all directions, searching for answers to what was happening while clinging to their mothers.

The ISIS militants looked at the women and laughed, cracking jokes, and mocking them. One of them said, pointing to the pile of scarfs, "I will sell you these for 250 dinars," which is a paltry sum, knowing that they did not have money.

Noor sat with her children in the corner of the room where they had been gathered. The room was very hot, and the presence of so many women and children in it was unbearable. Many of them vomited due to fear and extreme heat. Noor closed her children's eyes with her hands so that they would not feel afraid, but she failed. One of the girls quickly screamed, "I know you killed our men!" In a hysterical moment, she couldn't control her anger and ran towards the ISIS member to hit him, but another girl grabbed her and said, "Calm down! Anger won't do us any good now. They killed the men, but now we have to think about ourselves." The girl calmed down.

The ISIS member screamed, holding a gun in his hand, "Death will be the fate of any girl who screams again at her masters." He added, "Some food will be distributed to you, and whoever does not want to eat should dare to say so."

Potato chips, bread, and water were distributed to everyone. They had not eaten since morning and were then ordered to separate. Married women gathered in one part of the garden, elderly women in another, and unmarried girls in another corner. However, the little girls screamed and refused to be separated from their mothers, but they were forced and pushed away. Some of the young girls took the children of the married women as their own as if they had been mothers for their entire lives. This is what fear does to humans. However, Noor was lucky that her children were young, so they would go with her, but the boys were taken from their mothers and the girls as well. Everyone's face turned red from crying, knowing that a dark fate awaited them. As darkness fell, three large buses arrived, used by tourists travelling in Iraq. They placed the girls in two buses and the boys in another, and next to them were armored cars filled with ISIS members. They took them to where they did not know.

The number of different emotions that had gathered in those moments at that institute had made everyone freeze in their place without moving. Noor found herself with two children in a dark garden that differed in appearance from other gardens. She did not know why. Was it really different and only suitable for cold and dark nights, or was it something that made it sad and gloomy? She looked at the faces of everyone who remained there and saw extreme despair. At that moment, she realized that they did not fear death anymore after what had happened, and there was no light left in their eyes. Darkness as deep as the darkness spread by ISIS had taken hold of them. Her eyes widened in fear, and she said to herself, "Oh my God, they have succeeded in extinguishing the light within us, and now our souls are naked in the darkness, and our fate is destruction." After waiting for a while, buses arrived, carrying one bus elderly woman, promising to take them to places with air conditioning and delicious food. In another bus, woman with their children were taken, and each one went in a different direction. The bus that Noor was in with her children headed towards an unknown place, and there were some ISIS militants on the bus, wandering among the women. One of them approached Noor and placed his hand on her shoulder and then on her back, and he began to harass her. Each touch of his in front of her children was like a bullet piercing her pure body. Tears filled her eyes, and she asked her children to close their eyes, and she begged the ISIS member in a faint voice to leave her alone for the sake of her children. That was the first time she had heard the word "slave." The ISIS member said, "You are now a slave, and you belong to the Islamic State and the fighters, and we can do whatever we want with the slaves. So shut up, or you will be severely punished."

She cried bitterly without making a sound, not for fear of herself but for her children. She decided to accept the torment to stay with the children. The ISIS member touched her throughout the journey, as others did with the rest of the women. The bus was like a cemetery where life had disappeared, with sealed doors, silence prevailing, and darkness burying many beautiful hopes, silencing many free voices, and killing many souls. Then a call came to the bus driver that no one in the audience understood because he was speaking Turkmen. The bus stopped, the door opened, and a voice emerged from the darkness outside the bus, issuing loud and agitated orders to the fighters to evacuate everyone without causing any commotion. Everyone got off the bus without making a sound, not knowing where they were, but it was a large building that resembled a school. One of the women asked, "Where are we? And where are you taking us?" An ISIS fighter grabbed her shoulder forcefully and asked her to be quiet, but she later heard the fighter talking to another person that they were in "Tal Afar," a city with a Turkmen majority.

They did not feel afraid because they were in Iraq, and they were afraid of being taken to Syria. In Iraq, they had the opportunity to escape, which is what Noor also thought, holding her children's hands tightly and whispering to them, "Don't be scared ... we are safe here. Your father will come to save us." She looked into their eyes and found a glimmer of hope and light, so she rejoiced and vowed never to let that light go out.

They all headed towards the school and gathered in a hall where they felt extremely tired. Many of the children fell asleep as soon as they entered the hall, but the women could not even close their eyes due to the extreme tension. Some of them vomited due to severe mental pressure, and the place smelled of vomit and sweat. Then, ISIS fighters arrived with black garbage bags containing some bread and water, which they distributed to them so that they would not die of hunger, as they were now slaves of the Caliphate state.

Three painful days passed in that school, but Noor did not mingle with anyone. Her thoughts were with her children, and where the mind turned, the eyes followed. It was as if everyone was a ghost to her. She would have surrendered and killed herself a long time ago hadn't she wanted to protect her children.

A group of armed men came back and asked them to go out to the schoolyard, where buses were waiting to transport them to another place. At that moment, Noor panicked out of fear that they would be taken to Syria, but she heard a member of ISIS say they would be taken to Badush Prison in Mosul. She breathed a sigh of relief because she preferred being imprisoned in her own country rather than being transferred to another state. She took her children by the hand and calmly boarded the bus. After everyone got on, the buses moved along with armored vehicles protecting them, heading towards Mosul, where the Islamic caliphate was declared. Noor looked out the window at the barren lands, closed her eyes, and wished that all of this was a bad dream. But when she opened her eyes, she was still in that nightmare.

When the buses entered the city, Noor saw a bright sign that read, "Welcome to Badush." She had heard about the Badush prison in the news, when ISIS entered the city, they released all the criminals who were sentenced to prison there, which made her feel relieved that there were no more criminals there. Until they arrived at their desired location, the prison was very large and protected by barbed wire and massive concrete walls that smelled like crime. They were ordered to get off the buses and enter the prison, and they complied with the request and entered the prison yard, and silence prevailed over everyone. However, the ISIS member felt that something had to be said at that moment, so he grabbed the shoulder of one of the women and shouted, "You are now slaves; in other words, you are commodities for the Islamic State and the fighters, and you must serve them sexually because they are fighting for the sake of Allah and his messenger."

His speech ignited a fire in their souls, and their cries and screams filled that ominous prison. One of them shouted in Arabic, saying, "We prefer death to that! The Yazidi woman is pure and clean like a white sheet and should not be defiled by strangers," and she added in her mother tongue with tears streaming down her eyes and her hands raised towards the sky, "Oh God, send the angel of death to take our souls! Before any of these monsters touch us."

The ISIS member laughed provocatively and said, "Allah does not hear you, oh infidel ... Allah only hears the believers."

They were forcefully taken into the prison as they were too weak to overcome armed men, but now their fate was known. Noor, however, did not feel any fear. There was a great feeling inside her that told her what was happening was a violent dream that she would soon wake up from and laugh about with her husband. But she could not think about what would come without tension or panic. There and then, the trauma was obvious to her, she was confused.

At the same time, other ISIS members came and whispered among themselves, pointing their fingers at some of the women. At that moment, Noor learned they would select the women who would have sex with them. Her heart almost jumped out of her chest in fear. In a flash, she turned to the wall and put the dust from the ground on her face and hair, and bowed her head so they wouldn't notice her and wouldn't take her away from her children. But after less than five minutes, she felt an ISIS member approaching her. She could hear his footsteps, so she bent her head even further, feeling his hand touch her shoulder. She held her breath in fear, and her face became colorless. She closed her eyes tightly and held onto her children's hands. In those few seconds, more than a hundred scenarios of terror went through her mind, and each one is worse than the other. The man grabbed her shoulder, and she screamed, refusing to go with him. He hit her and beat her children mercilessly, stripping her of her clothes in front of her children while everyone laughed and pointed at her. The man raped her in front of them all. This was one of the worst scenarios she had imagined, but she heard a woman screaming beside her, and suddenly she was fully awake and didn't feel his hand on her again. She slowly opened her eyes and saw the woman next to her resisting and refusing to go with him. He grabbed her by the hair in front of everyone and said, "Anyone who doesn't come willingly will come like this. Do you understand, you cursed whores?"

The women and their children spent a week in that prison, witnessing inhumane acts every day. They took women every day without returning them. Fortunately, Noor wasn't one of them. The ordeal made them selfish, not thinking of anyone but themselves. But no one could blame the other because they were all in the same hell together.

At sunset, tensions rose again when an ISIS member approached and ordered the remaining women to follow him out of prison. Noor thought something terrible would happen and couldn't think of anything positive. As they left, buses were waiting for them, along with armored military vehicles filled with ISIS fighters. Noor whispered to her children to stay close to her no matter what happened. She sat in the back of the bus to avoid being noticed by the militants. After the bus was filled, it moved towards an unknown location again. Noor looked out the window and saw horses behind, which was the sun set, turning the sky a dark orange with other colors mixed in. This reminded her of the day she met her husband, whom she loved with all her heart, during the famous carnival (Ail Awal) that was held on the night of the Yazidi New Year, known as "Sarsali." The holiday celebrates the creation of the earth according to Yazidi belief, and they celebrate it with various kinds of festivities, including this carnival. In the past, men would ride their horses, and those who didn't own horses would ride donkeys. They would all race each other, and some would shoot guns and fireworks to welcome and celebrate the holiday. Women would cheer while wearing their best dresses, including white ones for older women and spring-colored ones for others, especially red, the color of the most famous rose that symbolizes the arrival of the holiday. It is a beautiful red rose called the April rose. They would then color boiled eggs, and some of the wealthy people would distribute the best types of fresh meat to the village. On the morning of the holiday, men would wake up and stick mud mixed with colored eggshells and April roses at their door to bring good luck and blessings.

The touch of the ISIS fighter on her leg made her wake up from her beautiful illusion and return to her bitter reality between the hands of a dirty ISIS fighter who harassed her all the way. Noor avoided looking at him so that he wouldn't feel that she was comfortable with his behavior. He continued to harass her until he moved on to another woman, and he continued to do so until they reached a vast city filled with the unfamiliar sound of the call to prayer, which most of them had only heard on television. The city was crowded with veiled women and men dressed in long Afghan robes without moustaches, carrying weapons as they roamed the city. The bus suddenly stopped in the middle of the city, and the driver spoke with another ISIS fighter. In the meantime, Noor saw a girl being brutally whipped with a whip until her back bled, and next to her was a crying child being whipped as well. The ISIS fighter noticed that she was looking at the violent scene and said to her, "This is the fate of anyone who violates the list of prohibitions established by the Sharia court."

He called one of the crowds out and asked him about the reason for their punishment. He said, "She did not comply with the Islamic dress code, and the child insulted one of the jihadists by calling them 'ISIS' instead of 'Islamic State soldiers.'" Noor asked him, in fear of being hurt, "What is the Islamic dress code?" He replied, "It is the hijab and niqab, which covers the entire body and face, and wearing black gloves as well."

Noor fell silent and said to herself, "Black like your souls." She wished she could say that to him to his face, but she did not have the courage to do so.

The buses continued until an hour passed, and they stopped in front of a large hall called "Galaxy Hall," guarded by a large number of armed men. They were ordered to get off and enter the hall. Noor got off with her children, and she bent forward in fear as she walked until she entered a wide hall with a high ceiling illuminated by lights. She saw a terrifying sight, took two steps back, and bumped into an ISIS fighter who pushed her forward with force and shouted angrily, "Move forward, you stupid woman."

She recoiled in horror and moved forward. The hall was filled with women, girls, and children, all from the Yazidi religion, and they were all up for sale. Dalal looked at her mother in amazement and asked about what she saw and when they would return home. Noor looked at her and, placing her hand on her cheek, hugged her in silence. Is it easy to remain silent when there is a raging volcano within you? No, such thoughts and pains cannot be borne alone, but Noor was forced to bear them. When she spoke again for her daughter, her voice was full of sadness, tiredness, and pessimism, and she said, "This is a play, and everyone here is an actor."

Dalal asked her, "But what does a play mean?" Noor replied, "They are filming the cartoon movies that you used to watch at home with your father ... and when this play ends, we will return home where your father is waiting for us eagerly." Dalal replied sadly, "But mother, I want to go home! I am tired here, and I miss my father."

Noor did not know what to say to a little girl who longed for her father, who used to spoil her. She decided to remain silent again when an ISIS member said to another, pointing at a girl, "I will buy this slave from you in exchange for a gun." The other ISIS member, feeling his hair and face, replied and laughed, "You are very generous." Noor remained in that hall, fearful that they would sell her with her children, but fortunately, she was not a striking beauty to attract attention. She was looking at the hall from a distant angle without anyone noticing her, even though she was up for sale with her children for one hundred dollars. The ISIS member who was offering them for sale shouted, "Gentlemen ... this is woman you will enjoy having sex with, and she will take her children to become your servants."

A man approached them, and Noor felt that this was the end, that if she was sold, she would lose everything, but the man looked at her face and laughed mockingly, saying, "Is this a woman or a monster?"

It is not common to see a woman rejoicing at being described as ugly, but inside her, there was joy and happiness that overwhelmed her, and her eyes sparkled with pleasure. When the ISIS militant walked away, she whispered, "I thank God for creating me ugly."

Meer heard his mother whisper and said, "But mother, you are not ugly!" Noor couldn't reply to her son due to the screams of three little girls being beaten because they refused to go with an ISIS prince. The princes and elders used to come to take the young and beautiful girls for rape, and when they were bored with them, they gave them to the armed men and got others. The virgin and beautiful girl was a prize for them, and when the militants were tired of them, they sold them to other militants. Those three girls could not resist anymore and got up from the ground with beautiful, innocent bodies covered with black cloth that did not even let sunlight pass through. How could it be fitting for a criminal to smell them and turn those virgin bodies into material bodies that are bought and sold!

The ISIS members continued to come to buy the girls, and a man came who was clearly wealthy. He requested to buy a group of girls and women, so the ISIS man asked him why he was buying a group. He replied, "I will buy them in bulk and offer them in public auctions in the markets."

The ISIS man agreed and sold him fifteen girls and gave him a girl as a gift for buying a large number. He was asked if he would like to stay until the draw for the beautiful and virgin girls so that he could get one of them for himself. He agreed to stay because he saw a beautiful girl and started looking and staring at her shape. The ISIS man numbered the girls and gave them Arabic names, writing those numbers on papers. Then he asked the attendees to draw the names. The trader received the number "four," but the girl he wanted was assigned to one of the armed leaders. He was afraid to object, but disappointment showed on his face, so one of the men asked him to sell him that girl in exchange for a phone credit recharge card. He refused and said, "I will sell her for a good amount in E-stores."

The man replied, "Gift her to one of the leaders, and you will receive his blessing, and your work will prosper."

He responded, "I don't know, I will see what I can do with her," and he took the girls and led them out of the hall towards endless nightmares.

Another man came and took five girls who were designated as the winners of the Quran memorization competition. Whoever succeeded in memorizing the Quran within a period specified by ISIS would receive a slave as a prize.

Six months passed in that hall in this way, until one night, ISIS members ordered the women and children who had not been sold to board a bus to be returned to Tal Afar. Noor felt terror that they would be killed because they were unwanted, so she planned to steal one of the ISIS members' phones and randomly call for help, but she knew it would not succeed. She then thought of asking to get off the bus to accompany her children to the toilet and escape but remembered that they were armed and would shoot them. So she surrendered to her reality and decided to face whatever might happen in Tal Afar.

The ISIS members distributed food to them since they were all very hungry. They ate all the rice and bread that was distributed to them. While they were eating, Noor noticed that it was taking longer than the first time they moved from Tal Afar to Mosul and immediately knew that they were headed to another location. Since she was afraid of what was about to happen and had nothing left to lose, she screamed loudly, "Where are you taking us? What are you going to do with us?" and suddenly lost consciousness. Everything turned black, but the strangest thing had not yet happened. Everyone on the bus felt dizzy and lost consciousness minutes after eating, and the bus did not stop that night and continued on its way to its destination.

After hours had passed, Noor woke up and found herself lying next to many other women in a dark room in a strange place. She looked around but did not see her children, so she jumped up in terror and ran outside the room. She saw her children playing outside with other children, they were in a house made of mud in the eastern style, with rooms adjacent to each other and a big garden. She looked at her children while deeply crying and moved towards them and called them, "Dalal ... Meer."

They turned to her and ran towards her, and she bent down, and opened her arms in front of them, laughing and crying. She hugged them tightly and stared into their eyes for a long time. Then, a member of ISIS came with an Arab-looking middle-aged man named Sheikh "Abu Osama." He ordered her to stand up and said to her, "You have been sold with your children to this man. Get ready to go with him." He threw a black veil over her and asked her to wear it with her daughter. Noor did not feel uncomfortable because her goal was to protect her children, so she obeyed his orders. She wore the veil and asked Dalal to wear that strange thing, although she did not want to. Her mother was able to convince her, and they got into an old, rundown "Opel Vectra" car with the man. She asked him in weak Arabic about the place where she woke up, and he replied, "We are in the capital of the Islamic State, Raqqa. At this moment, leave behind the world you were living in."

Noor leaned slightly to look through an unbroken part of

the front car window. She found nothing in front of her but a city that had lost peace and life, evil and death entered it, and there was nothing left but destruction, dust, and rubble. No civilians were seen, and everyone hid in their homes, fearing torture and kidnapping. All gone. All those outside were armed with a tough appearance, and there were no signs of life. However, nothing affected her more than a deserted shop clearly intended to sell tombstones. During the time of ISIS, there were only mass graves, and she learned then that she would not even get a decent grave if she died.

At every kilometer, there was an ISIS checkpoint. To cross it safely, one had to know the password they used between them. When approaching it, the Sheikh held her hand and said in a low voice that if they ordered her to say the password, she should say, "We support and endorse the Islamic State."

The car stopped, and the ISIS member put his head through the window, placing his left hand on the door, holding an AK-47 rifle in his other hand, and looking inside carefully. He asked the Sheikh, "Who are these?"

He replied, "They are my children and wife, and we belong to ISIS." He feared they would be taken away from him because he bought them with his money.

The militant gestured to another member on the other side to confirm the identity of the woman. He approached her and asked for the password of the Islamic State. Noor stared at him with frightened eyes and froze for a few seconds, then said, "We support and endorse the Islamic State." He nodded to him and said, "Let them pass." The sheikh shouted loudly and proudly, "Long live the Islamic State and its fighters!"

They continued their journey, passing through a city that was unsuitable for living; it was the land that protects evil and its victim at the same time until they reached a deserted house in an abandoned area that resembled the house where Noor woke up. A massive woman veiled from head to toe with black emotionless eyes was waiting for them at the door of the house, which made Noor think of the torture she would suffer with her. She closed her eyes for a moment, and when she opened them again, she saw the woman standing in front of her. Noor asked her anxiously, "How are you, my sister?" thinking that showing respect for her would make her more lenient, but she did not answer her and took Noor's children by the hand and went to the kitchen. Noor followed her, and she bent down in front of her, took her hand with both of hers, and asked her, "Please, my lady ... I will do whatever you ask of me, your servant or your worshipper, anything you want, but do not hurt my children."

She looked at her deeply and pointed to the dining table with her finger, and Noor, thinking that she had agreed to serve her, said excitedly, "What should I do, my lady? Should I clean up the place?"

A tall, dark-skinned girl with round, lifeless eyes, similar to the other woman, came and said despairingly, "She asks you to sit at the table and eat, she cannot say that because she is mute."

Noor was confused for a moment and could not believe it, so she looked at the woman as she threw her veil to the ground and took a deep breath, repeatedly as if she were drowning, and someone pulled her out before her breath was completely cut off. Noor was surprised by the beauty of her long silky black hair, her chocolate-coloured skin, and her symmetrical features as she stood looking at her. The girl asked her if she wanted to take off what she was wearing, and Noor responded hesitantly, "Is this allowed?"

The girl replied, "As long as your father is not here, you can do what you want. My mother and I don't care about what you wear."

Noor felt grateful to the girl and her mother and asked her hesitantly, "Why are you so kind to us?"

She sat at the table and began to eat without appetite and said, "We are not kind to you; we just don't harm you."

The girl was mature, much older than her age, carrying the responsibility of a mute mother alone and living with a violent father who didn't know the meaning of childhood.

Noor removed the veil from her head and Dalal's and sat hesitantly at the table. After what she had been through, it was difficult for her to believe that there was someone who did not want to harm her. She asked the girl with great tension to tell her the story of their lives and the reason for living under the rule of ISIS. The girl asked her about the reason for her curiosity, and she replied, "Because I am perplexed by your kindness."

The girl stopped eating and looked deeply into her eyes, with an end in sight, a storm in her head, and pain in her heart. She said, "I don't know where to start!" She paused for a moment and added, "My mother was not born mute, she became so because of the shock she experienced a month ago. On a very hot day, my father came with a girl the same age as me, fourteen years old. Her name was Rose; it is a Kurdish name which means the sun in Arabic. She looked a lot like her name. I still remember her yellow eyes, her long neck, and her distinctive smile. She was very beautiful! My mother took good care of her at my father's request. We had become used to her presence until that fateful night." She suddenly stopped narrating her story.

Noor asked curiously, "What happened that night?"

She said, "I don't know if you want to hear it, but since you keep asking me, I'll continue telling that story."

"Yes, please," replied Noor.

"On that night, my father brought one of the ISIS princes with nine armed men and ordered us to prepare a feast for them. We couldn't refuse because he was strict and stubborn. He would kill us if he got angry, and he would seize every opportunity to defame us in front of people and accuse us of betraying his family. He claimed that we refused to participate in the "Jihad Al-Nikah (Sexual Jihad)" and spy for ISIS."

Noor interrupted her to ask about her last words. "What do you mean by that last word?" Because she couldn't pronounce it. The girl replied, "You mean Jihad Al-Nikah?" Noor replied, "Yes."

The girl answered, "The organization has issued many fatwas to satisfy the sexual urges of the fighters, including considering whoever satisfies the fighters and helps them to discharge their sexual tension as a Mujahid (Jihadi). For them, Jihad is the ultimate goal, and man must be psychologically prepared for this Jihad for Allah! It doesn't matter how many fighters she has sex with in a day, as it is considered a Jihad."

"Why would Allah want a woman to do such a vile thing?" asked Noor in great surprise. "I don't understand that either," said the girl.

"Okay ... I'm sorry for interrupting you. Please continue," said Noor.

The girl continued, "I don't believe in religion. I see all the elements of existence in nature, and that's what makes me different from my father. But he doesn't know that, or else he would have killed me a long time ago. I won't reveal it to protect myself but rather to protect my mother. She's a very simple person who wants to live a peaceful life, but she hasn't succeeded in doing so because of her marriage to my father, who lives a noisy and complicated life. In this house that my father occupied, I grew up miserable, cowering every time he called me. But the presence of that girl was like living in a fantasy world because I had conversations with her that I had never had with anyone before. For example, one night, she asked me casually about my prince charming, and I didn't know what to say because I wasn't used to that. So, I asked her to talk about her own prince charming, if she wanted to. She smiled as if she was waiting for me to ask her and enthusiastically said that she didn't want a rich man or a state employee to take her to parties and upscale places, but rather a kind man who would care for her and be concerned about her details, just like her deceased father who, although poor, was like an angel who wanted to soar away in the sky of freedom and love. But my father and his colleagues had different opinions. That night, after we had eaten the food that my mother had prepared with our help, my father called me to the corridors of the house and asked me to bring Rose after dressing her in my prettiest dress. I wish I could have refused him back then, but didn't, because I was faced with two options: either do what he asked of me and save myself and my mother or refuse his request and face his violent anger. I was tired of seeing my poor mother being beaten and tortured, so I chose the first option and asked her to go to my father after wearing my blue dress. However, she refused to wear the blue color, and I didn't ask her about the reason because I wanted her to go to my father before he became angry with us. Can I ask you about the reason?"

Noor replied, "We grew up hearing stories about the genocides that our ancestors suffered in the past. I remember my grandmother's angry talk, saying that the Yazidis would face genocide again. She would say that every time we built a house after collecting money from doing agricultural work or hard daily work in the provinces of Kurdistan, where it was common among young people who had dropped out of school, we didn't believe anything she said, and we decided to live in the present without thinking about what might happen in the future. We heard from her that in the past, every Yazidi was forced to leave his religion at the hands of the Ottoman state, and they were made to wear a blue outfit as a symbol of their conversion to Islam, so it is not a desirable color for us."

"Okay ... I can understand it now," she said and added, "I lent her my chestnut dress, even though I didn't know why she refused the blue one. She put it on and went to see my dad. Five minutes passed without hearing anything, so I decided to go and see what was happening after another five minutes if I didn't hear anything. Time passed, and I was biting my nails from the extreme tension until Rose's scream shook the house. My eyes widened, and I ran to that room with my mom. I opened the door, and my dad was standing in front of me because he knew we would help her. He grabbed my shoulder angrily and asked me not to interfere in what didn't concern me, but I resisted him. With my height advantage, I saw behind his shoulder the dreams of that little girl being crushed under the feet of a filthy person who was raping her with all his brutality in front of everyone in the room while she was resisting, hitting, screaming, and crying all at once. I will never forget that moment when I looked at her; she was asking for help with her innocent eyes filled with extreme sadness. I saw in her eyes intense despair, as if the color of her eyes had turned black after the light inside them disappeared. I hit my dad in his genitals so I could help her, but when I passed through my dad, one of the armed men grabbed me, raised his gun in my face, and tied my hands and feet so I couldn't move. Then I saw my mom crying helplessly as she looked out the window. When the prince finished, he stood on his feet and said loudly and proudly that a non-Muslim girl had converted to Islam under his guidance, and with every provocation, he congratulated her on her good performance. He enjoyed raping a strong girl who resisted. Rose spat on his face, which angered him even more. He asked all the fighters to rape her, and then my mom screamed, refusing what was happening. Suddenly, she stopped screaming and fell to the ground. I begged them to let me check on my mom, but they didn't let me. I closed my eyes so I wouldn't see what was happening in front of me, but I couldn't help but hear moans mixed with suffering from a girl who was telling me about her dreams yesterday and was raped today in front of my eyes.

Tears poured from my eyes, and I jumped from my spot like I had been bitten by a snake. I felt something thick hit the back of my head, and I fell to the ground unconscious. I woke up to my mother's touch. That girl was lying on the ground in front of me, drenched in blood and her dress torn. I saw her withered breasts due to their harsh touch, and wounds covering her entire body from her resistance to what happened. Strands of her hair were scattered on the floor of the room. I concluded that they cut it to sever the thread of her life. Nothing compares to a girl's love for her hair. In that room, we lost against the injustice of life."

Noor learned that her fate would not be any better, yet she smiled at the girl and asked her not to forget what had happened. Life is not always unfair. The girl was amazed by Noor's strength, as she believed that life is always unjust for the different and the poor. If she believed in religion and the second one was not Yazidi, they would not have had to live all that violence, as people do not accept those who are not like them.

The evening had fallen when the door opened. Noor nervously felt her body with her hands. She jumped from her spot and held Dalal's hand, placing her behind her, fearing that they might attack her. They don't care about age; all they care about is that she is a female. The sheikh looked around the room, saying, "I have sold you to Abu Muawiya Al-Iraqi. A car will come early in the morning to take you to Iraq." And he left the room.

Noor looked at the girl happily, and then asked to hug her,

but the girl refused because she did not like emotional acts and did not believe that her father would not do anything for her after buying her, even if it was for one day. But she did not want to tell her that, so she remained silent.

Noor picked up her daughter and held her, saying, "I will kiss you now. You are five years old, so I will kiss you five times." Dalal laughed cutely and asked her to kiss her every year as she grew older. Her brother asked in surprise, "What if you die? How will she kiss you then?" She quickly placed her hand on her son's mouth and asked him to be quiet. Death is not something we joke about, and she promised them that they would stay together until the end.

After half an hour, they had prepared to sleep, and the sheikh entered the room and asked her to accompany him to his room. She didn't want to leave the room alone, but he refused to let anyone else accompany her and said, "Come alone, and hurry up."

For a moment, Noor realized that he was going to rape her that night. She felt sorry for herself and felt extremely lonely. Grief and sadness were her only friends in that room. She stood at the doorstep, and he ordered her to enter and sit next to him on the bed. She saw an old red chair in front of the mirror, so she sat on it, hoping he would leave her alone. She spoke to him in broken Arabic, saying:

"I am a mother of two children, and my husband was killed. I have nothing left but my honor, and I smell bad. I haven't bathed for over a month, my body is covered in hair, and my face is also ugly. Please let me go to my children."

He coldly replied, "Come and sit next to me ... then I will let you go." She stood on her feet and approached slowly. Then she shook her head left and right, refusing to do what was happening, and took a step back. He threatened her with her daughter, saying, "Do you want your daughter to be in your place?"

She froze in terror, she would agree to anything except harming her daughter. She asked, "What do you want me to do?"

He said, "I told you to come and kneel before me."

Noor knelt before him, and he held her chin and lifted her head. She looked away from him, but he insisted that she look into his eyes. He stared at her pale face, and in her grief, and great fear, he enjoyed what he saw before him. He got naked after removing his robe and took her hand, saying, "Come on ... please me."

He was an old man who could not perform sexually, and every moment with him was terrifying. Whenever she tried to distance herself from him, he pushed her forcefully. At that moment, the fear of death disappeared from her mind. Death is great, it does not come when we wish for it, but when we are in our happiest moments.

Humans do not understand the pain of a woman when she stands in front of a man who rapes her soul before her body. It is a painful tragedy written in the tears of her eyes.

PART III
CRIME & PUNISHMENT

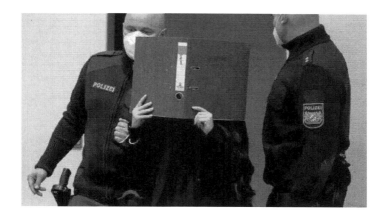

May 2015
12:15 PM, Al-Fallouja

She did not close her eyes even for a second all day long as she was heading with her children toward other days of slavery and captivity.

In those days, every Yazidi girl suffered a deep wound that would not easily heal, as things happened to them that they never imagined would happen in their own country.

Noor had no idea about the geography of the region. All she knew was that she was in a city whose name was always associated with fighting and bloodshed in American movies, which she watched clips of when her husband's friends came to visit. Her husband was a fan of war movies, but he never imagined living them in reality.

As the driver continued to monitor the road, he drove an old Toyota towards the west after they entered the city. It was a hot day, and Noor found it difficult to breathe with her niqab covering her face. She began to wonder to herself, "How will this new family be? I feel that we will suffer a lot with them!" She answered herself, "No! I don't think so. She may be a good woman who takes care of us well. I will serve her and take care of her, and in return, she will have pity on us."

Dalal asked her, "Mama ... I can't breathe in this thing, and I feel like I'm in the middle of the ocean. Please let me take it off." Noor replied, "Wait a little longer. You will take it off when we get home. A beautiful house with a green garden full of flowers and butterflies will be waiting for us..." Dalal interrupted her with excitement, "Are there butterflies too?"

"Yes, and delicious food and many cool sweets, like the ones we had in our old house."

"Okay. But I hate summer. When will winter come?"

"Soon, my love," Noor replied.

Dalal said happily, "In this winter, buy me a woolen sweater like the one our neighbor's daughter, Sarah, used to wear. Agree?"

Noor replied in a sad tone, "I will buy you everything you want, but bear with it for now."

The driver didn't leave the street until they reached the Jolan neighborhood where the family that bought them lived. It was noon prayer time, so the driver pulled over to the side of the road and got out of the car to pray. Noor was surprised by the huge number of mosques they passed by and the sound of the call to prayer that filled the city. At that moment, all sounds disappeared except for the voices of the Mullahs calling people to prayer and jihad. After the driver finished praying, he said in a voice that could be heard, "What a great feeling to be in the Islamic State and to be a resident of the City of Mosques," and then he instructed her to pray when she arrived at the house of the owner because he didn't have time to wait for her to pray there.

The neighborhood was miserable, poor, and dusty. It was difficult to leave the house due to the extreme heat, and just walking down one of its streets was enough to make your body and face burn and for sweat to pour out of you, soaking your clothes. But its residents had grown accustomed to this heat. In its old and dilapidated markets, men would drink tea and smoke cigarettes under the scorching sun, seeing it as a consolation for their worries and hardships that weighed them down throughout their lives.

The car stopped in front of an eastern house, and they got out of it exhausted from the long journey. The driver knocked on the door. When it opened, a tall, thirty-year-old dark-skinned man looked at them with a look of hatred. He had black eyes with thick eyebrows and light hair that he had not shaved, and he was wearing a brown robe with a beard. He shook his head and told the driver to "go away."

He instructed the others to enter the house. Noor learned that he was an ISIS member, Abu Muawiya, so she entered holding her children's hands. There was a woman at the end of the hallway looking at them with hatred. She didn't look like an Arab. She was a thirty-year-old blonde with blue eyes and harsh features, tall and wearing a black dress.

Abu Muawiya pointed to Noor and her children and said to the woman, "They are the captive and her children that I bought. Do whatever you want with them."

She replied, disgusted and putting her hand on her nose, "I know. They smell like the devil! What a nuisance they are."

She ordered Noor to come closer, so she grabbed her shoulder strongly and said with great nervousness, "I can't stand fools, especially if they are women and children, so be like inanimate objects when I don't order you to serve me." And she added, "I can't bear the names of the infidels from now on. Your daughter's name is Khadija, and your son's name is Omar, and you are Um Omar (the mother of Omar)."

"Okay, my lady," answered Noor, afraid.

She ordered her to go and cook, and in case she failed to serve a delicious meal, she would be punished severely. She was an extremely harsh woman who knew no mercy. Noor went to the kitchen and left her children sleeping on the floor as soon as they arrived because they were exhausted. The place smelled terrible as if they were living in a swamp. She started by cleaning the place first and then took two onions and placed them with a chicken on the stove. She cooked rice and prepared tomato and cucumber salad next to them on a large plate and brought it to their room, terrified that they might not like her food.

Um Muawiya watched her movements and noticed her thinness due to poor nutrition and hard work for her masters. Her chestnut dress, torn, made her feel very nervous. So, she asked her to put the food and leave the room quickly. She put the food in front of them, and Abu Muawiya looked at his wife and said angrily, "Jennifer, where is the bread?"

Um Muawiya shouted in anger, saying, "Damn you, you wretched woman, where is the bread?"

Noor's eyes widened in fear, and she said, "I'm sorry, my lady, I forgot it."

Um Muawiya glared at her with a look of malice and said, "You dirty mouse, did you forget it eats it?"

"No ... no, I swear I didn't eat it. I'll bring it now." Noor hurried to the kitchen and looked for the bread but couldn't find anything. She sat on the floor, frightened, and hugged her knees to her chest, thinking of a solution. At that moment, her daughter Dalal came in with bread in her hand, eating it greedily. Nora quickly took the bread from her, thinking of cutting it so that they wouldn't notice anything. But at that moment, Um Muawiya stood at the kitchen door and noticed the bread in Dalal's mouth. Noor froze in place and realized she would receive a harsh punishment.

She screamed at her, "You cursed liar!" and reached for the straw broom in the corner of the kitchen, grabbing it and gesturing, "Come here." Noor rushed to her daughter and begged, "Please, my lady, have mercy on my daughter. It's not her fault."

Um Muawiya grabbed Dalal by her hair amidst the screams of her mother and hit her with a broom, saying "I'll teach you a lesson you'll never forget." She added, "Oh my God, she's as stupid as her mother! They're like rats."

The little girl's eyes filled with tears as she put her head under her elbow and looked at her mother pleadingly. She repeated, "I was hungry."

However, Um Muawiya didn't stop hitting her. Noor rushed over and grabbed Dalal's hand, pulling her towards her and saying, "Please ... punish me instead. She's just a child and doesn't know anything."

At that moment, Abu Muawiyah entered and said in an angry voice, "I don't want to hear any noise in this house. Abu Osama will call me from outside the country." He added, "If you want to punish them, do it outside the house."

Um Muawiyah grabbed Noor by the hair and pulled her away, throwing her barefoot into the courtyard, where she stumbled on the ground covered with burning stones under the intense heat. She forced her to walk on them until sunset. She also forced her children to watch her suffer and warned them not to get close to her, or they would be beaten.

Noor stood on her feet, hungry and exhausted, but she kept that to herself, afraid that her children would suffer at the hands of that wicked woman. She felt her feet burning every time one of them touched the ground, she suffered and suffered, but she looked at her children and smiled at them, asking them not to get close to her in obedience to Um Muawiyah's orders.

Dalal looked at her innocently and asked, "Mom ... are you dancing?"

"Yes. Is my dancing beautiful?" she replied with a smile.

Dalal answered angrily, putting her hand on her head, "I was beaten, and my head hurts because she pulled my hair, and you're dancing!" And she added, "I'm also hungry."

Her brother replied, "I'm hungry too."

Her heart ached to hear that, and finally, despair overwhelmed her, so she shouted, "Oh my God ... oh my God!"

The world around her seemed like darkness, even though it was midday, and she felt she would never see the light.

Dalal noticed her mother's sadness and started crying.

Noor thought that Um Muawiyah surely heard her daughter crying, so she approached her and covered her eyes with her hands, saying, "Mommy will cry if Dalal don't laugh," but she couldn't convince her.

Fortunately, at that moment, Um Muawiya was busy eating and constantly whispering, "Stupid … stupid."

Beside her, Abu Muawiyah was on the phone with his friend, trying to convince him to join ISIS in Iraq, saying, "You will find all the pleasures of life here, from sex, and alcohol to killing, torture and money."

His friend asked, "What about my German nationality?"

He replied, "Travel to Turkey, and from there, enter Syrian territory. I will take you from there to Iraq to join us." He paused for a moment, thinking, and added, "My wife Jennifer is also German, but she is now a fighter in the Islamic State and holds an important position there."

The friend said, "I have been thinking about joining you since the announcement of the caliphate, but I could not convince my wife and children to follow."

Surprised, Abu Muawiya replied, "Does a man ask his wife's permission, or does he command her? You are becoming like the infidels because you live among them."

Angry, he said, "I did not mean that. If she does not agree, I will beat her and take her with me by force."

Abu Muawiya looked at Jennifer, a wicked smile on his face, and said in a low voice, "He fell into the trap."

Jennifer replied, exchanging the same wicked smile, "Oh, how I love stupid men."

Abu Muawiya said to his friend, "Well done, my fighter," and ended the call.

The night had fallen, and Noor continued to walk, leaving a trail of blood from her burnt feet. She struggled to breathe with cracked lips and eventually collapsed, unconscious. Tears streamed down her face as she thought of her hungry children, asleep on the ground, waiting for her punishment to end.

Her soul was about to leave her body when she was drenched with water from a bucket poured over her by Um Muawiya. The night breeze chilled her, and she shuddered, unable to stand on her convulsing legs. She heard the woman order Dalal to serve her and shout, "Khadija, bring hot water and soap to wash my feet."

Noor entered the house crawling, and Um Muawiya saw her in front of the door. She gave her a cat-like glance about to pounce on a poor mouse and said, "Oh, you are like a wounded dog!" Then she threw a piece of bread in front of her.

A strange silence befell her, and she put her head down on the ground and did not approach the bread despite her hunger. She had come to hate bread in that house and did not think of eating it again for the rest of her life.

Dalal came trembling, carrying a large bucket of water that was difficult for a girl her size to carry and placed it in front of her. However, she had put the soap in the water, causing it to spoil. She was still a young child who had not yet learned household chores, which angered Um Muawiya. She scolded and beat her, pouring hot water on her head, saying heartlessly, "I will burn you alive if you don't learn quickly."

She cried out in pain and screamed, "Dad, Mom, I'm burning!"

Her mother got up and headed towards that woman, taking a cigarette lighter from Abu Muawiya and setting it on fire. She angrily said, "You will burn in the fires of Hell just as you burn here." This is what she wished for in her imagination, but she could not do anything in reality, so she just cried and begged for mercy.

But her brother felt her pain and attacked Um Muawiya, hitting her with the soap bar and shouting, "Don't touch my sister."

At that moment, that child changed his fate. It was possible for him to survive with his mother, but his reaction made Abu Muawiya angry. He hit him mercilessly and decided to enlist him in ISIS and never let him return to that house again.

Noor was terrified. At first, she thought it was just a threat, but Abu Muawiya grabbed her son's shoulder and dragged him outside. He cursed him in the Iraqi dialect, saying, "politeless ... No manners." He added, "I will take you now to the night training camp, where you will receive special training. And don't ever think about coming back."

The nine-year-old child did not feel any fear. He said bravely, "You cannot touch my sister while I'm here ... I will always protect her."

Noor stood up in shock and ran towards Abu Muawiya. She sat on her knees in front of him and kept kissing his feet repeatedly. She begged him to leave her son, for she had nothing left in this world except her children, and she could not continue her life without them. She would spend most of her day with her husband and children, and when she left the house, she would return in less than an hour. She never made friends, and no one listened to her except her family.

With the reckless courage that Meer showed and the great hatred that accompanied Abu Muawiya's desire to send him away, this was how Abu Muawiya left the house, holding the boy's shoulder, without caring about the crying and pleading of his mother.

Noor was left alone with a crying girl on her lap. In one day, life threw all the weight of the loss of the dearest ones on her shoulders. She did not know what to cry for, whether for her husband, who was killed in his prime or for her poor son, who was taken away to an unknown fate. She wished for death every second she spent in that house. She could not bear what was happening, so she attacked Um Muawiya fiercely and started hitting her while crying and saying, "May God curse you ... Leave my children alone."

Um Muawiya's physical strength was much greater than hers, so she grabbed her by the neck with her big hands and said angrily, "I will kill you, you miserable woman."

Noor's face turned red, and she could hardly breathe. She said, "Please, kill me ... I beg you."

She looked at her intently and said, "I won't grant your wish ... I'll make you suffer." Then she hit her head against the wall, causing her to lose consciousness from the force of the blow.

The girl pressed her lips together, placing her small hands over them. She became motionless, like an object, afraid of being hit again, but she couldn't control the tears that remained on her face, covered in dust. Then Um Muawiya turned towards her and said, "Everything that happened is because of you, you little mouse."

It only took a few seconds before Dalal fled from the house to avoid being beaten, walking along the roads left and right. The darkness had descended, and she couldn't see well, but she continued to run without stopping. She didn't realize she had moved far away from home due to her intense fear, but in a moment of realization, she stopped moving and panicked, folding in on herself. However, she felt someone was watching her, so she stuck to the wall to avoid being seen and closed her eyes, sitting in the darkness. The wind blew, carrying the dust of the city, and she heard the rustling of the sad and eerie tree branches. The child trembled, and her fear and terror intensified. Suddenly, she heard faint sounds approaching her location, and she surrendered to her fate, her heart beating strongly and violently.

It was only a matter of minutes before a pack of stray dogs passed close to her. She opened her eyes and stared at the dogs, thinking to herself that they were better than Um Muawiya because they wouldn't harm her as that woman did. However, it was only a few seconds before she heard those sounds again, and she realized they weren't the sounds of dogs. She turned to the source of the sounds on her left and saw two veiled women carrying weapons. She thought they would pursue their own path like stray dogs, not realizing that nobody would hurt her except for Um Muawiya. But they approached her little by little, and their voices rose as they ordered her to stand still without moving. The girl was terrified, hoping that someone would save her at that moment, but to no avail. One of them looked at her intently and said, "We've caught a mouse for Um Muawiya."

Her skin crawled with fear and terror. She darted to the right and ran with all her might, her instinct urging her to turn around. The two thin women were no more than a meter away from her, and she panicked until her knees couldn't carry her anymore. One of them grabbed her dresses and said in a low voice, "If you don't stop, I will feed you to the dogs."

She was still moving like a fish in the woman's hand, feeling that she was lifted off the ground, and the dress's collar began to choke her. The more she moved, the tighter the collar got around her neck, so she stopped moving, and her face showed signs of exhaustion from running.

They took her to the house of Um Muawiya, where she was waiting for them. Dalal ran towards her mother, who was still lying on the ground unconscious and hugged her. As soon as Um Muawiya saw her hugging her mother, she went crazy, looked at her sternly, and ordered her to come closer. Dalal backed away a little in fear and panic.

Then the wretched child approached her voluntarily, thinking that she would comply with her orders so that she would not be severely punished. But Um Muawiya had a different opinion. She decided to whip her a hundred times for attempting to escape from her mistress. Um, Muawiya was participating in armed patrols in Fallujah as a policewoman in the "Diwan Al-Hisba" or the morals police, punishing women who violate ISIS's instructions in brutal ways that do not occur to innocent people.

But one of the policewomen stepped forward indifferently and said, "The best thing to use is the biting tool."

The other one approached and glared at the girl with an evil look, saying, "Let the girl choose her punishment."

Um Muawiya took the girl's hand and ordered her to choose her punishment, saying, "Whipping or biting tool?"

She had no idea what they were talking about, but she answered fearfully, "The biting tool." She thought it was a lighter punishment than the one Um Muawiya suggested, who was the most wicked woman she had ever seen in her life.

Um Muawiya asked that policewoman if she had the biting tool, and she replied, "Yes, it's with me." She revealed a set of sharp iron teeth from under her cloak and put it in her mouth. Um Muawiya pushed the girl towards her, and she grabbed her and started biting her arms and shoulders, causing her severe pain. Delal screamed and tried to escape, but in vain. She was crying for help on the ground and it was a few minutes when her body was covered in wounds and blood.

That night, while she was being beaten and bitten, she thought of the girl she had seen in a movie with her father. The girl was her same age and had been rescued by the German army after her father's ship had sunk, and she had been left alone on an island in the middle of the sea. She felt that she would be able to escape from her own bitter reality just like that girl had to ease her pain. She wondered if there was anyone who would save her.

This desire was a candle that illuminated her world, but within minutes she returned to reality and collided with the fact that no one would save a poor girl like her.

Dalal spent five days unconscious, semi-naked, on a dirty, worn-out bed, embodying deprivation, pain, and misery. She was stripped of her childhood without anyone grieving for her except her mother, who woke up to her daughter's wounds. She had difficulty speaking from the force of the blow. She worked for Um Muawiya during those days without saying a word, afraid that her sick daughter would be thrown into the street. She took care of her daughter and put water in her mouth, kissing her forehead to keep her warm so she wouldn't get cold and succumb to death.

While she was lost in her thoughts, she suddenly heard a faint voice filled with exhaustion saying, "Mama." She turned to Dalal's bed and saw her opening her eyes by force. She took the small hands between hers, with tearful eyes, and asked, stuttering, "My little one ... are you okay?"

The little girl collapsed in tears as she felt her wounds, so her mother gave her a glass of water to drink, but she couldn't manage to hold it as her hands trembled from weakness, causing the water to spill on the ground. However, her mother tried to give her hope so she could overcome reality. She stroked her hair, which she had not washed for a long time, with her hand and said in a heavy voice, "My beautiful daughter, your brother is back, and he's in the courtyard playing with the chickens and goats, waiting for you to play with him."

Dalal asked, "Did my brother come back?"

Her mother replied, "Yes, and if he saw you crying, he would leave again."

"Well, I won't cry, but there are no chickens and goats in this house," said Dalal.

Her mother smiled and said, "Your father brought them here so you could play with them."

The little girl didn't believe it, but she chose to believe it because that's what she wanted the most. She started crying again, not out of frustration or anger but out of pain and agony.

That day was one of the hottest days in May, with the temperature exceeding fifty degrees. Um Muawiya returned angry from her daily tour in the "Diwan al-Hisba." She entered the house and heard Dalal crying, so she went crazy and shouted loudly, "What is this annoying sound?"

Noor's heart was racing, and she ran to Um Muawiya and said, "I'm sorry, ma'am ... she is in a lot of pain. I'll make her sleep now."

"It's better for both of you to make her stop, or else I know how to make her stop," Um Muawiyah replied and continued, "Bring water and wash my feet."

Dalal couldn't hold back her crying and said to her mother, "I'm in pain."

"This evil woman will punish you," her mother said.

"What will she do next?" Dalal wondered.

"I'm afraid she'll send you away from me," her mother said, and tears streamed down her eyes.

But the little girl's pain was great, and she couldn't sleep or stop crying, no matter how hard her mother tried. Um Muawiya came to the room where Dalal was lying, her eyes filled with anger. She shouted at her, "You stupid little mouse, stop crying," and grabbed her injured shoulder. She continued screaming, "I'll hit you if you don't stop crying."

The little girl was frightened, so she stopped crying, but she wet her bed, and the urine got to Um Muawiya's foot, so she became very angry, shouting for Abu Muawiya, "Get rid of this dirty mouse ... I can't stand her in my house."

Abu Muawiya was even eviler than her, and he would do anything she asked, no matter how big it was, without even batting an eyelid.

He came with an iron chain in his hand and said, "Since you came to this house, we have never had any peace." He took the girl from her bed to the courtyard. Noor threw herself on her daughter, thinking she would take the beatings for her and bear her suffering, but Abu Muawiya took the little girl by the hand and threw her close to the window on the ground. He said to her mother, "If you get closer to her, I will shoot you." He tied her to the window without food or water.

Noor shouted, "Sir, please, have mercy on her, she won't annoy you anymore."

He put his finger between her eyes and said, "Shut up, or I will tie you with her."

Noor fell between the claws of these two monsters, suffering for her daughter's torment as she watched from afar, crying, screaming, and feeling the pain. But in the end, she surrendered her daughter's fate to God, fearing that if she did something, they would kill the girl.

The five-year-old girl entered a struggle with her own soul, preventing it from abandoning her body, even though she would finally see peace. She did not think about her hunger and thirst but rather about her mother. How can a hungry child facing death think of anyone but herself and possess this strength?

Then she thought to herself, "Why does she keep calling me a mouse? Is it because I am an ugly child or because I am small in size? My father used to call me 'my little one,' so I think it's because I am small." She was in pain every time Um Muawiya called her a mouse.

Five days passed, and Dalal was eagerly awaiting salvation as her mother was watching her from behind her tears and smiling.

Darkness fell after a long day, and delusions began to dominate her mind. She saw her father around her, shining with a halo of light in front of the courtyard door, looking at her with a smile. She wanted to call him, but she could not. She tried, again and again, to stand on her feet and go to him, but she could not. He came closer to her little by little, and she smiled with great difficulty. She felt his soft hand touching her cheek and playing with her hair, feeling safe as she had not since long ago, and fell into a deep sleep.

Dawn broke, and she opened her painful eyes and looked around, but she saw no one but her mother lying in the courtyard in front of her, like the other days. She felt that her chest had become heavier and her breath harder, but she did not want to give in to her weakness. She distracted her mind from her pain and thirst and saw a courtyard decorated with beautiful greenery, colorful butterflies dancing joyfully among the flowers, and goats and sheep eating grass. She envied them deep in her heart for their abundance of food, and the warm sun embraced the earth and brought with it a cold breeze that entered the folds of her beautiful dress. Her father came with her brother, holding her hand and smiling, lifting his hand before her, asking her to accompany them on their journey. She stood on her feet, ran toward them, and fell into a deep sleep.

When the sun rose, Um Muawiya approached the girl, but she didn't move. She stepped back and said in a loud voice, "The mouse is dead. I don't want to see her body when I come back," and went out to the street.

That day was not like any other day—the baby girl died. She lived a short life that began at the end of the night and ended at the beginning of the day, enduring hunger, thirst, and beatings in order to live a life like other children. She was like an angel shining in the light and disappearing in the darkness, and she became a beloved guest awaited by the angels.

Noor got up from her place and walked slowly towards her daughter's body. Shivers ran through her body as she trembled with fear, and she ran towards her, embracing her to her chest and screaming like a wounded animal. Her scream echoed throughout the city, but only God could truly hear it.

She closed her tear-filled eyes, and her soul trembled inside her. With a voice filled with pain, she cried out, "My child has died! My little one has died!" Then she screamed loudly, then laughed, then began to sing, and finally collapsed crying, kissing every part of her daughter's body and saying, "I waited for your birth for so long with your father, and your presence was like the moon that illuminated the darkness of our nights. What will I do now? My moon has disappeared! Your body is full of wounds, your clothes are torn, and your stomach is empty! How will I forgive myself for your death in this way?"

Darkness took over her soul, for when a person loses a loved one, they wonder how the sun can rise on time, people can walk on the streets, children can play, the elderly can listen to the radio, and the television can broadcast news bulletins that report on the world's disasters, but they do not report on their own disaster!

October 25, 2021
Munich

The court was formed, and the lawyers, the prosecutor, and the judges sat down. The judge asked the accused to stand up and requested her to say her final words.

Um Muawiya stood up and looked at the court as if she was innocent and unaware of the reason for her trial. She said, "I tried to convince Abu Muawiya by all means not to kill her, but I was a slave like that girl and her mother. I was afraid that if I tried to save her, that man would kill me. I am regretful for everything, and these are my final words."

The prosecutor asked, "How were you a slave and tried to return from Germany to areas still controlled by ISIS?" Um Muawiya replied, "I was afraid that I wouldn't get my rights here."

The prosecutor responded, "Do you have rights in ISIS, and would you not have rights in a country like Germany?"

Then, the prosecutor requested that the court hear the testimony of the little girl's mother. The judge accepted the request and asked Noor to provide her testimony. She stood up and resisted until she managed to control herself while seeing the deception and lies that Um Muawiya was telling. She said with a heavy voice, "She and her husband killed my little daughter without feeling any guilt. My daughter died of thirst while they looked at her every morning and evening after tying her to the chains of their home's window. I wanted to bury her, but they prevented me from doing so. My daughter did not even get a grave in this life because of them. Instead, they have taken her to an unknown place. They forced me to serve them after killing my daughter, and they forced me to pray while knowing that I am an yazidi. After all this suffering, they sold me to an ISIS member named 'Abu Sabah,' who practiced all kinds of torture and sexual abuse on me. One of them sold me to another until, after a long battle in Tal Afar, I left with the displaced people to the Kurdistan region." She continued, crying, "This woman is responsible for my daughter's death. I beg you to punish her with the most severe punishment."

The prosecutor stood up and asked the court, "You have heard everything, and all the evidence that proves the conviction of Jennifer, also known as Um Muawiya, has been presented to you. Therefore, I request that she be convicted with the most severe punishment."

The five judges stood up, along with everyone in the courtroom, and the chief judge said loudly, "Jennifer J., after reviewing all the documentary evidence and witness testimony, the court has decided to find you guilty and sentence you to ten years in prison for aiding and abetting crimes against humanity, including slavery and incitement to the war crime of attempted murder by omission, and joining a foreign terrorist organization." He continued, "You have the right to appeal the sentence within the time period specified by the law."

Um Muawiya looked at her hands, then at the ceiling of the courtroom, feeling her face and hair. She said, "This is unfair."

Noor exclaimed triumphantly, "No judgment in the world will bring back my daughter, but how happy I am today! After six years, my daughter will finally rest in peace. The one who killed her will receive her punishment in the depths of the prisons."

The End

Summary of what happened after the events of the story

Months after the trial of Um Muawiya, Abu Muawiya was sentenced to life imprisonment in Germany for the same crime, and his punishment was welcomed by the Yazidi community. However, the Yazidi community did not see Um Muawiya's punishment as fair and demanded a stronger punishment that would be proportional to the crime she had committed.

The fate of Meer, son of Noor, is still unknown, but all indications lead to his death.

Many Yazidi girls and children are still missing, and those who have been freed live in difficult conditions in tents, while another part of the survivors have been transferred to Germany to receive psychological treatment.

Large waves of displacement occurred towards the Kurdistan region after the ISIS attack, and until the time of writing this novel, most of them were still refugees in tents.

Some have migrated to the United States, Europe, and especially Germany by passing through the Aegean Sea that connects Turkey and Greece, which led to the death of many of them as they searched for freedom and safety.

Some returned to Sinjar after it was liberated from ISIS, but they live in difficult conditions under the Turkish shelling for the entry of PKK forces into the city and the absence of a unified administration.

Therefore, the Yazidis continue to describe their situation in a phrase, saying, "We are like a chickpea, hit by a stone."

ABOUT THE AUTHOR

Suzan Khairi Khedher is a novelist whose passion for storytelling is deeply rooted in her experiences as a lawyer and as a member of the Yazidi community. Born and raised in Sinjar town in Iraq, Suzan was profoundly impacted by the tragic events of August 3, 2014, when her people faced genocide. This harrowing experience inspired her to use her voice and pen to shed light on the plight of her community and to explore themes of resilience, survival, and hope in her writing. In her debut novel, *The Gift of the Feast*, Suzan delves into the complexities of human nature and the quest for redemption in the face of adversity. Through richly drawn characters and vivid prose, she invites readers on a journey of self-discovery and transformation.

Suzan Khairi Khedher's commitment to amplifying marginalized voices extends beyond her writing. As an alumna of the International Visitor Leadership Program (IVLP) in the USA in 2019, she has actively engaged in cross-cultural dialogue and advocacy for human rights. Her dedication to fostering understanding and empathy has been recognized with the honorary citizenship of Nebraska state in the USA.

In addition to *The Gift of the Feast*, Suzan has penned another compelling novel titled *Thirst*, which shines a light on the harrowing experiences endured by Yazidi girls in the captivity of ISIS. To stay updated on Suzan Khairi Khedher's latest projects and to connect with her, visit these social media platforms:

 Suzankhidher@gmail.com

 @KhairiSuzan

 Suzankhairi

 Suzankhairi

Policy Studies Organization Resources

The Policy Studies Organization (PSO) is a publisher of academic journals and books, sponsor of conferences, and producer of programs. There are numerous resources available for scholars, including:

Journals
Policy Studies Organization publishes dozens of journals on a range of topics:
Arts & International Affairs
Asian Politics & Policy
China Policy Journal
Digest of Middle East Studies
European Policy Analysis
Latin American Policy
Military History Chronicles
Popular Culture Review
Poverty & Public Policy
Proceedings of the PSO
Review of Policy Research
Indian Politics & Polity
Journal of Elder Studies
Policy & Internet
Policy Studies Journal
Policy Studies Yearbook
Politics & Policy
World Affairs
World Food Policy
World Medical & Health Policy
World Water Policy
Risks, Hazards & Crisis in Public Policy
Ritual, Secrecy, & Civil Society
Saber & Scroll Historical Journal
Sculpture, Monuments, and Open Space (formerly Sculpture Review)
Sexuality, Gender & Policy
Security & Intelligence (formerly Global Security & Intelligence Studies)
Space Education and Strategic Applications
International Journal of Criminology
International Journal of Open Educational Resources
Journal on AI Policy and Complex Systems
Journal of Critical Infrastructure Policy
Journal of Indigenous Ways of Being, Knowing, and Doing
Journal of Online Learning Research and Practice

Conferences
Policy Studies Organization hosts numerous conferences, including the Middle East Dialogue, Space Education and Strategic Applications, International Criminology Conference, Dupont Summit on Science, Technology and Environmental Policy, World Conference on Fraternalism, Freemasonry and History, AI – The Future of Education: Disruptive Teaching and Learning Models, Sport Management and Esport Conference, and the Internet Policy & Politics Conference. Recordings of these talks are available in the PSO Video Library.

Yearbook
The Policy Yearbook contains a detailed international listing of policy scholars with contact information, fields of specialization, research references, and an individual scholar's statements of research interests.

Curriculum Project
The Policy Studies Organization aims to provide resources for educators, policy makers, and community members, to promote the discussion and study of the various policies that affect our local and global society. Our curriculum project organizes PSO articles and other media by easily serachable themes.

For more information on these projects, access videos of past talks, and upcoming events, please visit us at:

ipsonet.org

Related Titles from Westphalia Press

The Limits of Moderation: Jimmy Carter and the Ironies of American Liberalism by Leo P. Ribuffo

The Limits of Moderation: Jimmy Carter and the Ironies of American Liberalism is not a finished product. And yet, even in this unfinished stage, this book is a close and careful history of a short yet transformative period in American political history, when big changes were afoot.

The Zelensky Method by Grant Farred

Locating Russian's war within a global context, The Zelensky Method is unsparing in its critique of those nations, who have refused to condemn Russia's invasion and are doing everything they can to prevent economic sanctions from being imposed on the Kremlin.

Sinking into the Honey Trap: The Case of the Israeli-Palestinian Conflict by Daniel Bar-Tal, Barbara Doron, Translator

Sinking into the Honey Trap by Daniel Bar-Tal discusses how politics led Israel to advancing the occupation, and of the deterioration of democracy and morality that accelerates the growth of an authoritarian regime with nationalism and religiosity.

Notes From Flyover Country: An Atypical Life & Career by Max J. Skidmore

In this remarkable book, Skidmore discusses his "atypical life and career," and includes work from his long life in academe. Essays deal with the principles and creation of constitutions, anti-government attitudes, the influence of language usage on politics, and church-state relations.

The Athenian Year Primer: Attic Time-Reckoning and the Julian Calendar
by Christopher Planeaux

The ability to translate ancient Athenian calendar references into precise Julian-Gregorian dates will not only assist Ancient Historians and Classicists to date numerous historical events with much greater accuracy but also aid epigraphists in the restorations of numerous Attic inscriptions.

Siddhartha: Life of the Buddha
by David L. Phillips,
contributions by Venerable Sitagu Sayadaw

Siddhartha: Life of the Buddha is an illustrated story for adults and children about the Buddha's birth, enlightenment and work for social justice. It includes illustrations from Pagan, Burma which are provided by Rev. Sitagu Sayadaw.

Growing Inequality: Bridging Complex Systems, Population Health, and Health Disparities
Editors: George A. Kaplan, Ana V. Diez Roux, Carl P. Simon, and Sandro Galea

Why is America's health is poorer than the health of other wealthy countries and why health inequities persist despite our efforts? In this book, researchers report on groundbreaking insights to simulate how these determinants come together to produce levels of population health and disparities and test new solutions.

Issues in Maritime Cyber Security
Edited by Dr. Joe DiRenzo III, Dr. Nicole K. Drumhiller, and Dr. Fred S. Roberts

The complexity of making MTS safe from cyber attack is daunting and the need for all stakeholders in both government (at all levels) and private industry to be involved in cyber security is more significant than ever as the use of the MTS continues to grow.

Female Emancipation and Masonic Membership:
An Essential Collection
By Guillermo De Los Reyes Heredia

Female Emancipation and Masonic Membership: An Essential Combination is a collection of essays on Freemasonry and gender that promotes a transatlantic discussion of the study of the history of women and Freemasonry and their contribution in different countries.

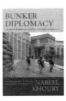

Bunker Diplomacy: An Arab-American in the U.S. Foreign Service
by Nabeel Khoury

After twenty-five years in the Foreign Service, Dr. Nabeel A. Khoury retired from the U.S. Department of State in 2013 with the rank of Minister Counselor. In his last overseas posting, Khoury served as deputy chief of mission at the U.S. embassy in Yemen (2004-2007).

Managing Challenges for the Flint Water Crisis
Edited by Toyna E. Thornton, Andrew D. Williams, Katherine M. Simon, Jennifer F. Sklarew

This edited volume examines several public management and intergovernmental failures, with particular attention on social, political, and financial impacts. Understanding disaster meaning, even causality, is essential to the problem-solving process.

User-Centric Design
by Dr. Diane Stottlemyer

User-centric strategy can improve by using tools to manage performance using specific techniques. User-centric design is based on and centered around the users. They are an essential part of the design process and should have a say in what they want and need from the application based on behavior and performance.

Masonic Myths and Legends
by Pierre Mollier

Freemasonry is one of the few organizations whose teaching method is still based on symbols. It presents these symbols by inserting them into legends that are told to its members in initiation ceremonies. But its history itself has also given rise to a whole mythology.

How the Rampant Proliferation of Disinformation has Become the New Pandemic by Max Joseph Skidmore Jr.

This work examines the causes of the overwhelming tidal wave of fake news, misinformation, disinformation, and propaganda, and the increase in information illiteracy and mistrust in higher education and traditional, vetted news outlets that make fact-checking a priority

Anti-Poverty Measures in America: Scientism and Other Obstacles
Editors, Max J. Skidmore and Biko Koenig

Anti-Poverty Measures in America brings together a remarkable collection of essays dealing with the inhibiting effects of scientism, an over-dependence on scientific methodology that is prevalent in the social sciences, and other obstacles to anti-poverty legislation.

Geopolitics of Outer Space: Global Security and Development
by Ilayda Aydin

A desire for increased security and rapid development is driving nation-states to engage in an intensifying competition for the unique assets of space. This book analyses the Chinese-American space discourse from the lenses of international relations theory, history and political psychology to explore these questions.

Contests of Initiative: Countering China's Gray Zone Strategy in the East and South China Seas
by Dr. Raymond Kuo

China is engaged in a widespread assertion of sovereignty in the South and East China Seas. It employs a "gray zone" strategy: using coercive but sub-conventional military power to drive off challengers and prevent escalation, while simultaneously seizing territory and asserting maritime control.

Discourse of the Inquisitive
Editors: Jaclyn Maria Fowler and Bjorn Mercer

Good communication skills are necessary for articulating learning, especially in online classrooms. It is often through writing that learners demonstrate their ability to analyze and synthesize the new concepts presented in the classroom.

westphaliapress.org

Printed in Poland
by Amazon Fulfillment
Poland Sp. z o.o., Wrocław